ŠEVČÍK
Op. 1 Part 1

SCHOOL OF TECHNIQUE

SCHULE DER TECHNIK

ÉCOLE DE TECHNIQUE

for

VIOLA
(ALTO)

arranged / bearbeitet / arrangées

by   von   par

Lionel Tertis

Cover picture: an important viola by Giovanni Paolo Maggini,
c.1600-1610. Photograph from Christie's of London.

Bosworth

REMEMBER!

(1) The first consideration in string playing, is the attainment of *perfect intonation.* This can only be achieved by the most *intense* and *concentrated* listening, (not superficial listening). *Never* pass a note that is the slightest degree out of tune.

(2) *Hold* and *keep* your fingers down on the strings in all these exercises, whenever and wherever it is at all possible.

(3) Attention must be paid to accurate note *values.* Be particularly careful when there are two notes with *separate* bows, immediately followed by two notes of the same value in one bow, or one note separately, followed by three notes of the same value in one bow etc. etc. No matter how varied the groupings, every note must be of exact equal value.

(4) When practising these exercises *slowly* lift your fingers high and feel you are doing so from the *knuckles* and bring your fingers down hard on the fingerboard,—when practising them *rapidly,* do not lift your fingers high and put them down *lightly* on the fingerboard.

(5) Divide the bowing up so as to, *first,* practise the exercises slowly and play them in tune. When you can do this efficiently, use the bowing as indicated, or as many notes in the one bow as possible.

NOTICE

(1) La première qualité qu'il faut s'appliquer à obtenir, lors de l'étude de tout instrument à cordes, est la *justesse d'intonation.* Celle-ci ne s'acquiert qu'au prix d'une attention *soutenue* et *concentrée* (pas d'attention superficielle). Veillez donc à ce que chaque note soit rigoureusement juste sans faire la plus minime concession à la médiocrité.

(2) Au cours de ces exercices *posez* et *maintenez* les doigts bien appuyés sur les cordes partout où la chose est possible.

(3) Observez minutieusement la *valeur* des notes. Veillez y spécialement lorsque deux notes avec coups d'archet *séparés* se trouvent être suivies de deux autres notes de même valeur mais figurant dans un même coup d'archet, ou lorsqu'une note isolée est suivie de trois notes de même valeur dans un même coup d'archet, etc.. Les diverses façons dont les notes peuvent être groupées importent peu, pourvu qu'à chacune d'elles il soit toujours donné sa valeur adéquate.

(4) Commencez par jouer ces exercices *au ralenti* et faites en sorte que les doigts s'élèvent très haut. Il faut vraiment sentir que tout le travail se fait dans les charnières des *articulations.* Abaissez ensuite avec force les doigts sur le manche. Lorsque, par la suite, vous jouez ces exercices en un tempo plus *accéléré,* levez les doigts moins haut et abaissez les sur le manche avec plus de légèreté.

(5) Répartissez vos coups d'archet de manière à jouer d'abord ces exercices en un tempo assez lent mais toujours avec une intonation rigoureusement juste. Dès que vous serez à même de jouer de la sorte avec aisance, accélérez et conformez-vous aux indications des coups d'archet tout en vous appliquant à jouer le plus de notes possibles en un seul coup d'archet.

ZUR BEACHTUNG

(1) Von vordringlicher Wichtigkeit für das Spielen auf Streichinstrumenten ist *untadelig-saubere Intonation.* Diese kann nur erreicht werden durch intensiv-konzentriertes (niemals oberflächliches) *Hören.* Lass keinen Ton durchgehen, der auch nur im geringsten unrein in der Stimmung ist.

(2) Lass bei diesen Übungen die *Finger auf der Saite liegen,* soweit und solange es möglich ist.

(3) Achte auf genaue *Notenwerte,* besonders wenn auf zwei *einzeln gestrichene* Noten unmittelbar zwei *gebundene* Noten gleichen Wertes folgen — oder auf eine einzeln gestrichene Note drei gebundene gleichen Wertes usw. Ganz gleichgültig, wie die Notengruppen auf den Bogen verteilt sind: Stets muss jede Note genau den ihr zugehörigen Wert erhalten.

(4) Beim *langsamen* Üben die Finger hoch (aus dem Knöchelgelenk) aufheben und energisch auf das Griffbrett aufsetzen—beim *schnellen* Üben nur wenig aufheben und locker aufsetzen.

(5) Studiere die Übungen *zuerst langsam* mit sauberer, schöner Tongebung, dann erst halte dich an die angegebenen Bögen oder spiele auf einen Bogen so viel Noten wie möglich.

PREMIERE PARTIE
PREMIERE POSITION

Exercices sur une corde
Il faut répéter chaque mesure plusieurs fois, d'abord lentement, puis plus vite en lié et en detaché.

FIRST PART
FIRST POSITION

Finger-exercises on one string
Repeat each bar several times, slowly, then quickly, and alternately legato (tied, connected) and staccato (detached, separated).

ERSTER TEIL
ERSTE LAGE

Fingerübungen auf einer Saite
Man wiederhole jeden Takt mehrere Male, langsam und schnell gebunden und gestossen.

1 *

Les demi-tons 1r et 2e doigt Corde de RE

Semitone 1st to 2nd finger D String

Halbton zwischen 1. und 2. Finger, D-Saite

Also to be played thus:
Peut se jouer également comme suit:
Auch so zu spielen:

* Recommencez le présent exercice sur chaque corde.
** Laisser les doigts en place.

* Practise this No. on each string.
** Hold the fingers down on the string.

* Übe diese Nr. auf jeder Saite.
** Die Finger auf der Saite liegen lassen.

2 *

Demi-ton: 2.-3. doigt.
Corde de Sol

Semitone: 2nd to 3rd finger.
G string

Halbton: 2.-3. Finger.
G-Saite

* Travaillez ce No. sur chaque corde. | * Practise this No. on each string. | * Auf jeder Saite üben.

3*

Demi-tons:	Semitones:	Halbtöne:
0-1., 3.-4 doigt.	0 to 1st and 3rd to 4th fingers.	0-1., 3.-4. Finger.

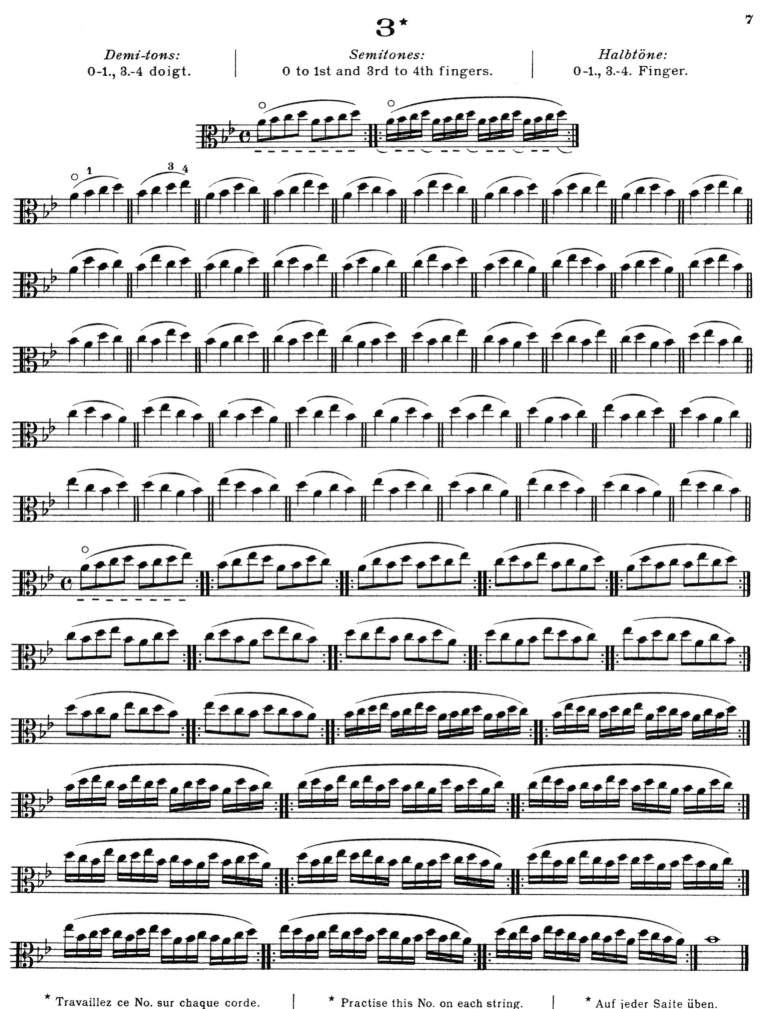

* Travaillez ce No. sur chaque corde. | * Practise this No. on each string. | * Auf jeder Saite üben.

B. & Co. Ltd. 21508a

4

On répète d'abord une mesure, puis deux mesures ensemble.

Begin by repeating each single bar and then the same in groups of two bars.

Man wiederhole zuerst zu einem Takte, dann zu zwei Takten.

5

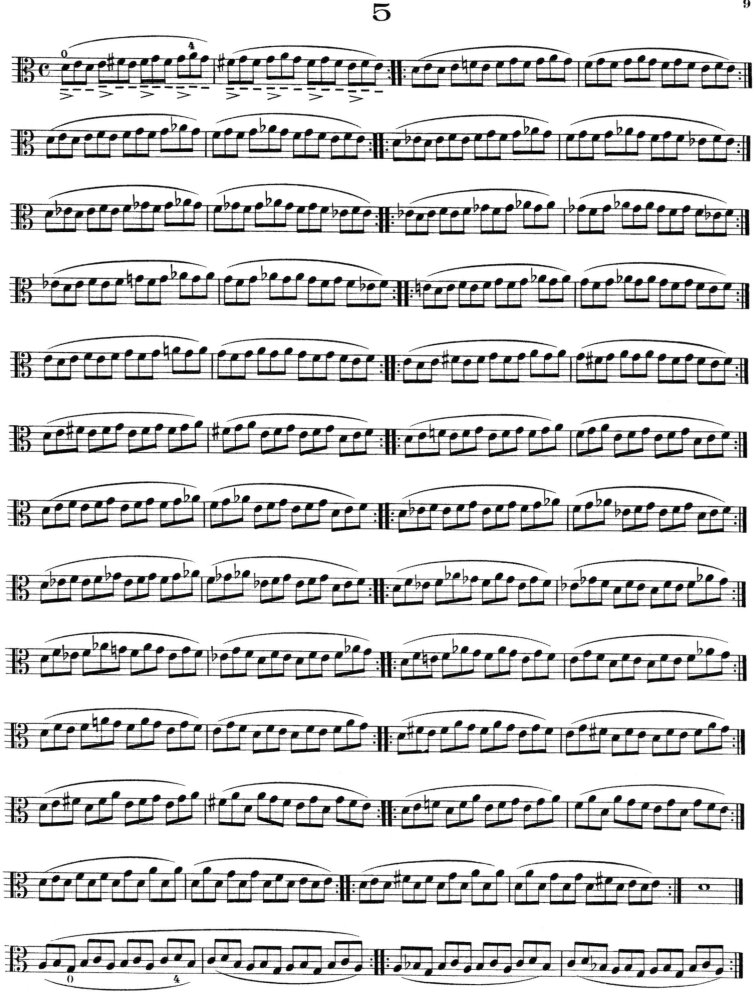

B.& Co. Ltd. 21508a

7

Maintenez les doigts abaissés partout où la chose est possible. Excellent moyen pour obtenir l'extension progressive des doigts.

Keep your fingers down where possible, to help finger stretches.

Die Finger möglichst liegen lassen — als Stütze für Streckung und Spannung.

9

10

Exercices sur deux cordes
On répète d'abord une mesure, puis deux mesures ensemble.

Exercises on two strings
Begin by repeating each single bar, then in groups of two bars.

Übungen auf zwei Saiten
Man wiederhole zuerst zu einem Takte, dann zu zwei Takten.

Dans cet exercice, il faut, avant tout, viser à passer d'une corde à une autre sans que l'on puisse remarquer le moindre changement de sonorité. Dans la pratique il faut en arriver à un jeu tellement homogène que l'on ait réellement l'impression d'entendre jouer le tout sur une seule corde.

The endeavour in this exercise must be to cross the strings very carefully from one to another with the bow, without any suspicion of accent. In fact, at the actual crossing it should sound as near as if you were playing on one string.

In dieser Übung ist sorgfältig auf den Bogen=Übergang von einer Saite zur anderen zu achten. Es darf dabei keinerlei Akzent zu hören sein, die Übung muss vielmehr klingen, als ob sie auf *einer* Saite gespielt würde.

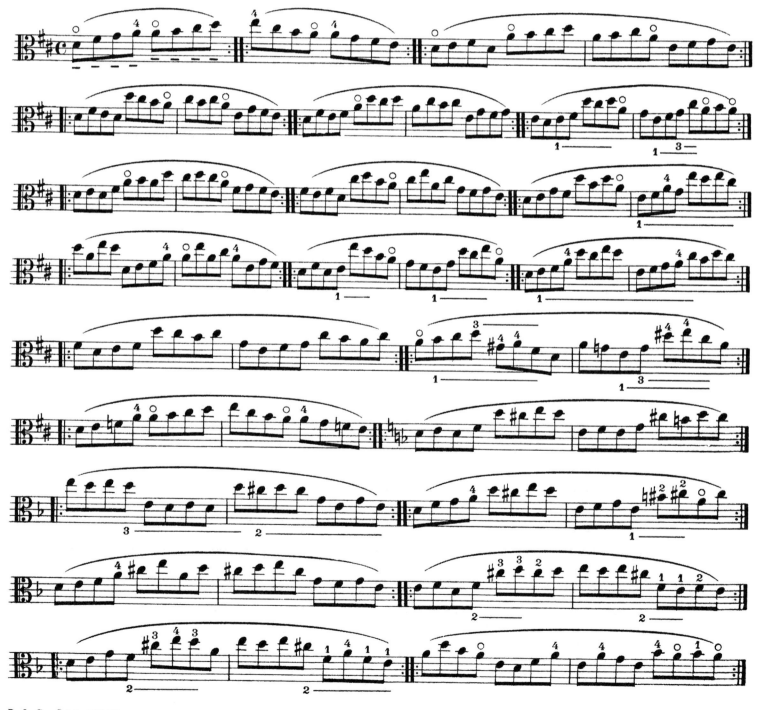

18

Maintenez les doigts sur les cordes partout où la chose est possible. | Keep your fingers down wherever possible. | Finger liegen lassen, soweit es möglich ist.

B.& Co. Ltd. 21508a

11

Exercice du poignet droit
Cet exemple doit être exécuté par chacun des coups d'archet suivants.

Exercise for the right wrist
This example must be practised in each of the following styles of bowing.

Übung des rechten Handgelenkes
Dieses Beispiel ist mit allen folgenden Stricharten auszuführen.

Exemple
Example
Beispiel

Cet exercice avec les différents coups d'archet peut se jouer sur les cordes de Do et de Sol (en Do majeur) et celles de Ré et de La (Ré majeur.)

This exercise with the various bowings to be also practised on on C and G strings (in C major) and D and A strings (in D major.)

Diese Übung ist mit den verschiedenen Stricharten auch auf der C= und G= Saite (in C=dur) und auf der D= und A= Saite (in D=dur) zu üben.

Coups d'archet   *Bowing-Styles*   *Stricharten*

12

B.& Co. Ltd. 21508a

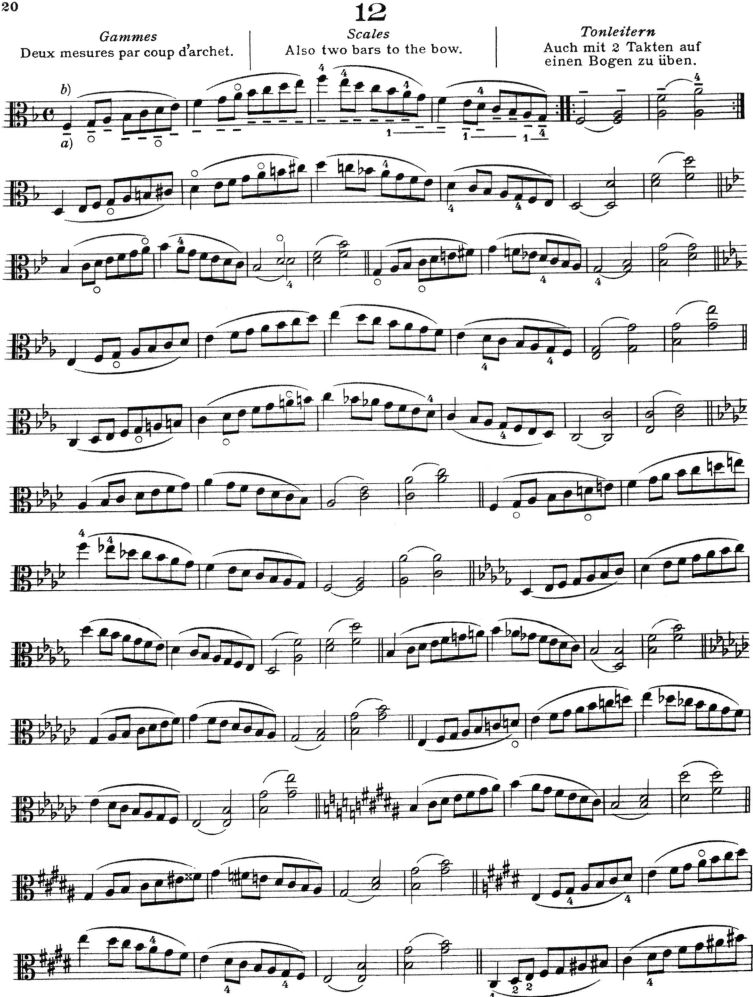

Gammes
Deux mesures par coup d'archet.

Scales
Also two bars to the bow.

Tonleitern
Auch mit 2 Takten auf einen Bogen zu üben.

13

Gammes en tierces	*Scales in Thirds*	*Tonleitern in Terzen*
Les signes ♯, ×, ♮, placés en parenthèse, reçoivent leur signification seulement en répétant les gammes mineures.	The Sharps(♯), double-sharps (×) and naturals, or cancelling-signs,(♮) shown in parenthesis are only applicable when practising the minor scales.	Die eingeklammerten Zeichen ♯,×,♮, sind nur bei der Wiederholung der einzelnen Moll - Tonleitern zu beachten.

MAJOR — MAJEUR — DUR

MINOR — MINEUR — MOLL

14

Exercice en sixtes
★ Observez les indications de doigté de la parenthèse lorsque vous jouez les noires en sixtes.

Exercises in Sixths
★ Use fingering in parenthesis when played as crotchet sixths.

Übung in Sexten
★ Benutze den Fingersatz in Klammern, wenn du die Sexten in Viertelnoten übst.

15

Octaves
Maintenez les doigts abaissés aussi longtemps que possible. Faites cet exercice avec le 1r et le 4e doigt uniquement.

Octaves
Keep Fingers down as long as possible. Practise this exercise also with 1st and 4th finger only.

Octaven
Die Finger so lange wie möglich liegen lassen. Übe diese Etüde mit nur 1. und 4. Finger.

24

16

Neuviémes, dixièmes etc.
Laissez les doigts sur les cordes
aussi longtemps que possible.

Ninths, Tenths, etc.
Keep the fingers down on the
strings as long as possible.

Nonen, Decimen, u.a.
Die Finger sind, wo möglich,
liegen zu lassen.

17

Accord parfait. | Triad (major.) | *Dreiklang.*

18

Tout cet exercice doit être éxé-
cuté par chaque coup d'archet désigné.
Sp. De la pointe
Fr. Du talon } de l'archet.
g.B. Tout l'archet

The whole of this exercise must
be practised in each of the pre-
scribed styles of bowing.
Sp. at the point
Fr. At the heel
g.B. Whole length of bow.

Diese Übung ist mit jeder Strich-
art ganz auszuführen.
Sp. An der Spitze
Fr. Am Frosch } des Bogens.
g.B. Mit ganzem Bogen.

B.& Co. Ltd. 21508a

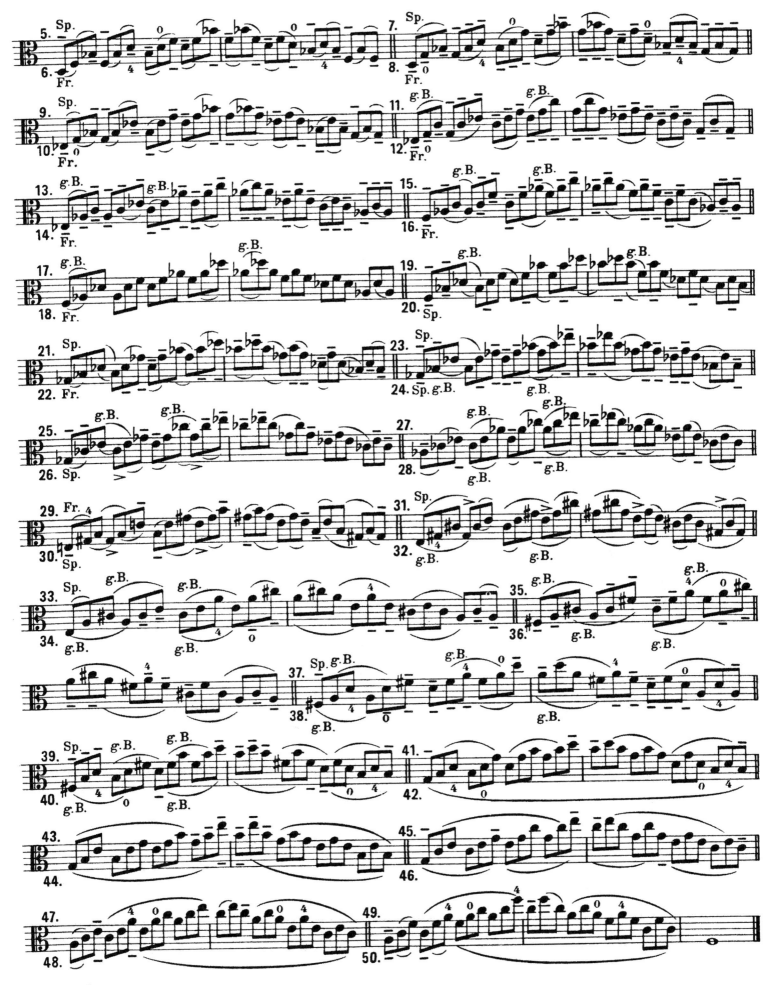

26

19

Gamme chromatique.
Faites cet exercice *posément* avec une *forte* pression des doigts.
Faites cet exercice *rapidement* avec une *légère* pression des doigts.

The Chromatic Scale.
Practise *slowly* with *great* pressure of fingers.
Practise *fast* with *light* pressure of fingers.

Chromatische Tonleiter.
Übe *langsam* mit *festem* Fingeraufsatz.
Im *raschen* Tempo mit *leichtem* Fingeraufsatz.

20

The Chord of the Diminished Seventh.
Hold down semibreves (without sounding them) wherever this is at all possible.

Verminderter Septimenaccord.
Die in ganzen Noten angegebenen (nicht zu spielenden) Fingeraufsätze sind durch den ganzen Takt liegen zu lassen.

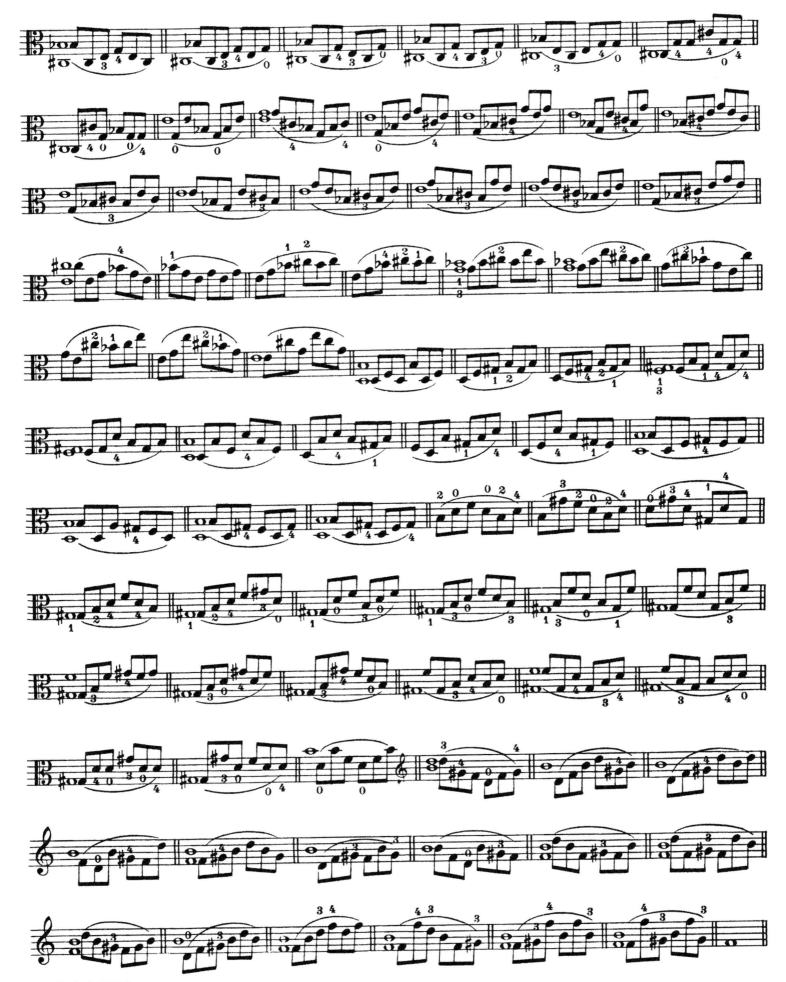

21

22

Divers accords arpégés | *Various arpeggiated (broken) chords* | *Verschiedene Accorde arppeggiert*

32

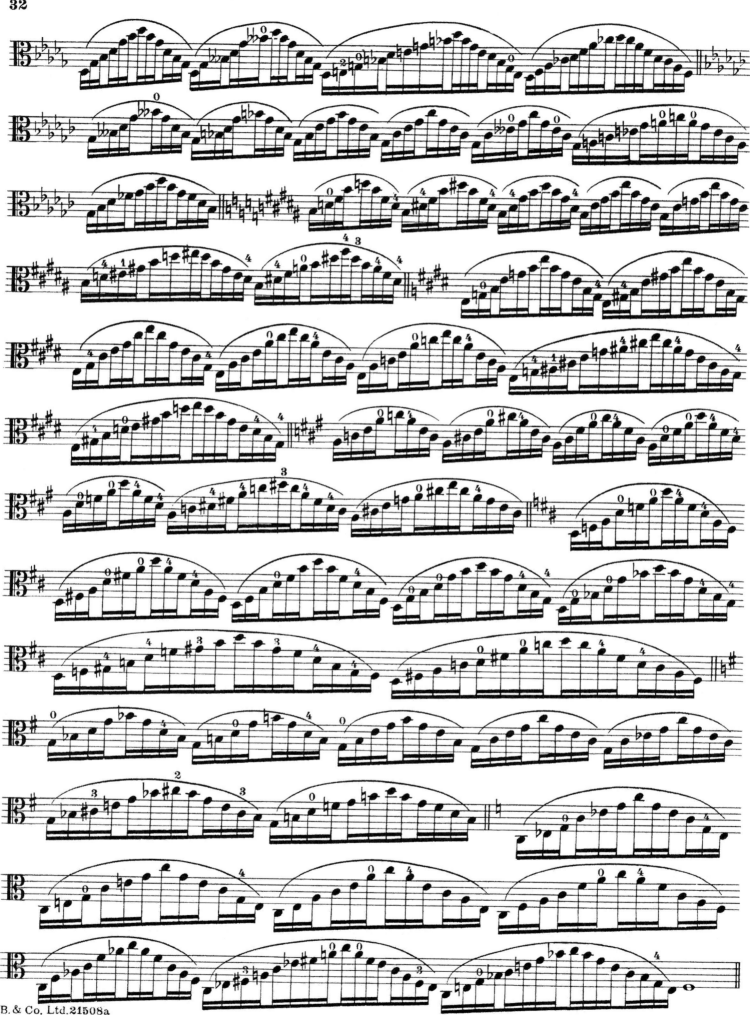

B. & Co. Ltd. 21508a

23

| *Exercices en doubles notes* | *Exercises in Double-stopping* | *Übungen in Doppelgriffen* |

| La ronde doit être *strictement maintenue* dans le ton aussi bien que les noires. | The semibreve must *remain perfectly* in tune as well as the Crotchets. | Die ganzen Noten müssen *im gleichen* Ton wie die Viertel=noten ausdruckslos = gleich-mässig klingen. |

24

25

26

Exercice des différents coups d'archet.

Explication des signes.

Sp.	De la pointe	de l'archet
M.	Du milieu	..
Fr.	Du talon	..
Fr.z....Sp.	Du talon jusqu' à la pointe	..
Fr.z....M.	Du talon jusqu' au milieu	..
M.z....Sp.	Du milieu jusqu' à la pointe	..
h.B.	La moitié	..
g.B.	Tout l'archet.	

Exercises in various Styles of bowing.

Explanation of the Signs.

Sp.	At the **point**	
M.	In the middle	
Fr.	At the heel **or** nut	
Fr.z....Sp.	From the heel right to the point	
Fr.z....M.	From the heel to the middle	
M.z....Sp.	From the middle to the point	
h.B.	Half bow-length	
g.B.	Whole bow-length	

Übung in verschiedenen Stricharten.

Erklärung der Zeichen.

Sp.	An der Spitze	des Bogens
M.	In der Mitte	..
Fr.	Am Frosch	..
Fr.z....Sp.	Vom Frosch bis zur Spitze	..
Fr.z....M.	Vom Frosch bis zur Mitte	..
M.z....Sp.	Von der Mitte bis zur Spitze	..
h.B.	Mit halbem Bogen.	
g.B.	Mit ganzem Bogen.	

Employez le métronome pour ces différents coups d'archet.

Practise these various bowings with a metronome.

Übe diese Bogenstrich-Varianten mit Metronom.